Pessimisimo
The Art Of Negative Thought

Aubrey Malone

Published in the UK by
POWERFRESH Limited
Unit 3, Everdon Park,
Heartlands Industrial Estate,
Daventry
NN11 5YJ

Telephone   01327 871 777
Facsimile   01327 879 222
E Mail info@powerfresh.co.uk

Copyright © 2004 A.D. Malone
Cover and interior layout by Powerfresh

ISBN   1904967019

All rights reserved. No part of this publication may be reproduced or transmitted in any form or by any means, electronic or mechanical, including photocopying, recording or any information storage and retrieval system, or for the source of ideas without the written permission of the publisher.

Printed in Malta by Gutenberg Press Ltd
Powerfresh September 2004

Aubrey Malone, was born in Co Mayo in 1953. He moved to Dublin in 1969, attending Belvedere College and then UCD where he studied English and Philosophy before going on to become a teacher. He published a short story collection, Flight, in 1980. Since then he has worked mainly in journalism, having been a feature writer and reviewer of movies and books for most of the national newspapers and magazines at one time or another on a freelance basis. Married, he lives in Dublin.
Amongst Aubrey's numerous publications are: Hollyweird (Michael O'Mara books), a compilation of Hollywood-related trivia; The Brothers Behan (Blackhall), a biography of Brian and Brendan Behan; the best-selling The Cynic's Dictionary (Prion); Historic Pubs of Dublin (New Island); and a biography of Ernest Hemingway, Hemingway: The Grace and the Pressure (Robson Books), Little Books The Big 40, 50, 60 as well as Turning 18 (Powerfresh).

This book is dedicated to anyone who ever saw the glass half empty, who thinks every silver lining has a cloud attached to it who thinks of funerals when they see flowers, who's life is an infectious disease, and who realises that the light at the end of the tunnel is more often than not a train coming the other way.

Don't tell your friends about your indigestion. 'How are you' is a greeting, not a question. *(Arthur Guitarman)*

I run the 'Daily Express' purely for propaganda. *(Lord Beaverbrook)*

A lie can travel round the world while the truth is putting on its boots. *(Mark Twain)*

If you keep crossing and uncrossing your legs like that, you'll set yourself alight. *(Kenneth Tynan to a nervous friend)*

'Marriage is lonelier than solitude.' *(Adreinne Rich)*

I couldn't believe the number of people outside the palace on the Queen Mother's (85th) birthday. If the woman had died there would have been less. And I'd have been hammering the nails into the coffin to make sure she'd stay in there. *(Morrissey)*

I love mankind. It's people I can't stand. *(Charles Schultz)*

What negroes want is tight pussy, loose shoes, and a warm place to shit. *(Earl Butz)*

You know the problem with men ? After the birth, we're irrelevant. *(Dustin Hoffman)*

'I haven't laughed so much since my husband,died.' *(Anon)*

Sex to Peter Rachman was like cleaning his teeth - and I was the toothpaste. *(Christine Keeler)*

'The wages of sin is alimony.' *(Carolyn Wells)*

Nice guys finish last. *(Leo Durocher)*

I don't understand anything about ballet. All I know is that during the interval the ballerinas stink like horses. *(Anton Chekhov)*

I've often wondered how businessmen used to cope before mobile phones were invented. How did they tell their wives they were on the train? *(Pete McCarthy)*

A little grovelling bastard. *(Spike Milligan on Prince Charles on live TV. He followed the comment up with a fax to the Prince himself, with the words: 'I suppose a knighthood is out of the question?' He actually did receive one in 2001, the year before he died).*

Aren't women prudes if they don't, and prostitutes if they do? *(Kate Millett)*

Prince Charles is an insensitive, hypocritical oaf and Princess Diana is a selfish, empty-headed bimbo. They should never have got married in the first place. I blame the parents. *(Richard Littlejohn)*

It's better to be wanted for murder than not to be wanted at all. *(Marty Winch)*

Give a man a free hand and he'll run it all over you. *(Mae West)*

When Anne Boleyn said to Henry the Eighth 'Not tonight darling, I have a headache', he replied, "We'll soon fix that'. *(Mike Harding)*

At the last magician's show I attended, there was an unfortunate lapse in concentration during his 'Sawing the Woman in Half' routine. Fortunately the mishap didn't prove fatal, and the lady concerned is now living contentedly in Scarborough and Devon. *(Denis Norden)*

My father died of cancer when I was a teenager. He had it before it became popular. *(Goodman Ace)*

All bad philosophers have a certain influence; good philosophers never. *(Bertrand Russell)*

Television is a medium of entertainment that permits millions of people to listen to the same joke at the same time and still be lonesome. *(T.S. Eliot)*

There's plenty of men that can't sleep in peace at night unless they know that they've shot somebody. *(Sean O'Casey)*

When people come to talk to you of their aspirations, count the spoons before they leave. *(Logan Pearsall Smith)*

When vices give us up, we flatter ourselves that it is we who are giving them up. *(Duc de la Rochefoucauld)*

Princess Margaret and the rest of them should be pitied more than despised, because they're prisoners of an outdated, archaic and pointless institution called the monarchy. It would have been a mercy to them if Cromwell had cut off a few more heads and made sure that the royal line stopped on the chopping block a few centuries ago. *(Terry McGeehan on the death of Princess Margaret in February 2002)*

Never trust anyone who wears a beard, a bow tie, two-toned shoes sandals or sunglasses.*(Michael Caine)*

Only my modesty allows me to cope with my perfection. *(Eddie Irvine)*

We used to build civilisations; now we build shopping malls. *(Bill Bryson)*

My wife's best friend has just celebrated the 20th anniversary of her 29th birthday. *(Kevin Goldstein-Jackson)*

We can forgive those who bore us. We cannot forgive those whom we bore. *(Duc de la Rochefoucauld)*

Adam was a rough draft. *(Erica Jong)*

I only kill in self-defence. I mean, what would YOU do if a rabbit pulled a knife on you? *(Johnny Carson)*

I've always realised that if I'm doing well at business I'm cutting some other bastard's throat. *(Kerry Packer, former chairman of Consolidated Press Holdings)*

Brains are never a handicap to a girl if she hides them under a see-through blouse. *(Bobby Vinton)*

I know nothing about sex because I was always married. *(Zsa Zsa Gabor)*

In business we cut each other's throats, but now and then we sit around the same table and behave, for the sake of the ladies. *(Aristotle Onassis)*

I come from an environment where, if you see a snake, you kill it. At General Motors, if you see a snake, the first thing you do is hire a consultant on snakes. *(Ross Perot)*

He treated everyone the same. He was an equal opportunity destroyer. *(Eddie Fisher on his doctor Max Jacobson)*

Justice must not only be seen to be done - it must be seen to be believed. *(J.B. Priestley)*

It takes a certain courage and a certain greatness to be truly base. *(Jean Anouilh)*

The reason I don't think Jeffrey Archer should have gone to jail is because now he's going to have even more time to write. *(Paddy Murray on Archer's conviction for perjury and perverting the course of justice in 2001)*

Nobody really trusts anyone. Otherwise, why do they put 'tilt' on a pinball machine? *(Steve McQueen)*

A moron with less on. *(Totie Fields on Raquel Welch)*

I may be your father, but you sound like a son of a bitch to me. *(Ernest Hemingway to a stranger who called him 'Papa' in the street one day).*

Why on earth do doctors drink so much? I suppose it gives them something to do while they're smoking. *(Pete McCarthy)*

No man thinks there is much ado about nothing when the ado is about himself. *(Anthony Trollope)*

Many of them didn't know they were deaf until they heard it on the radio. *(Kirn Bielenberg on Irish army deafness claims)*

All animals are equal, but some are more equal than others. *(George Orwell)*

If you are foolish enough to be contented, don't show it. Grumble with the rest. *(Jerome K. Jerome)*

My pet hate is nouvelle cuisine. The kitchen staff stand back saying 'Enjoy, enjoy' and I find myself staring in disbelief saying 'Find, find'. *(Chris Tarrant)*

The Civil Service has a difficulty for every solution. *(Lord Samuel)*

My father always told me, 'Own the land you live on. Then you can piss on it without being arrested'. *(Richard Harris)*

Policemen aren't there to create disorder. They're there to preserve disorder. *(Richard Daley)*

A man who hates dogs and loves whiskey can't be all bad. *(W.C. Fields)*

There's only one thing in the world worse than being talked about and that's NOT being talked about. *(Oscar Wilde)*

I've never liked clowns at circuses. They were the only thing in the world that actually made you look forward to the Mongolian jugglers. Why should anyone with ludicrous make-up, bizarre hair and ridiculously loud clothes assume they're going to make people laugh? If they did, we'd all go to the big top every Christmas to see Barbara Cartland top the bill. *(Chris Tarrant)*

The message of our age is that you have to fuck the guy next door in order to succeed. *(Eamon Dunphy)*

I don't want people in my face. I'm having three-months off on holiday. I want to stay home and pick my nose. *(Noel Gallagher in 1996)*

Hard work never killed anybody, but I figure, why take a chance? *(Charlie McCarthy)*

Santa Claus has the right idea: visit people once a year. *(Victor Borge)*

Sigmund Freud was the greatest villain that ever lived, a man worse than Hitler or Stalin. *(Telly Savalas)*

According to obituary notices, a mean and useless citizen never dies. *(Clarence Darrow)*

The good die young because they see it's no use living if you've got to be good. *(John Barrymore)*

When a man forgets his ideals he may hope for happiness, but not till then. *(John Oliver Hobbes)*

If it were necessary to tolerate in other people everything that one permits oneself, life would be unbearable. *(Georges Courteline)*

We should all learn to take things easily - especially other people's things. *(Harry Graham)*

The greatest pleasure I have known is to do a good action by stealth and have it found out by accident. *(Charles Lamb)*

A pleasant feeling is always generated by the demise of a celebrity. The occasion gives us nonentities a lot to discuss, and it provides us with situations upon which to lavish those tears which our sons and lovers find embarrassing and try to prevent us from shedding. *(Quentin Crisp)*

Advertising is the science of arresting human intelligence long enough to get money from it. *(Stephen Leacock)*

I went to my doctor and asked him for something for persistent wind. He gave me a kite. *(Les Dawson)*

A major part of my life has been spent in that state of resentful coma which at universities is called research. *(Harold Laski)*

No man is born prejudiced against others, but every man is born prejudiced in favour of himself. *(David Stafford Clark)*

History teaches us that men behave wisely when they have exhausted all other alternatives. *(Abba Eban)*

Experience is what you have left after you've forgotten her name. *(John Barrymore)*

Scruples are things that tell us to go ahead and do the right thing after we've considered doing the wrong thing and concluded it wasn't worth the risk. *(L.L. Levinson)*

Immorality is the morality of those who are having a better time than we are. *(H.L. Mencken)*

My window cleaner was a lethargic menial with all the sensitivity of the Berlin Wall. *(Woody Allen)*

Hell hath no fury like a hustler with a press agent. *(Frank Sinatra)*

No one will ever convince me that Ms isn't short for mistake. *(Jim Davison)*

Those who think it permissible to tell white lies soon go colour blind. *(Austin O'Malley)*

For God's sake don't say yes until I've finished talking. *(Darryl F. Zanuck)*

A drunkard is like a whiskey bottle - all neck and belly but no head. *(Austin O'Malley)*

If I say that he's extremely stupid, I don't mean that in any derogatory sense. *(Alan Bennett)*

I was up in Camden market and I saw this guy and he wasn't wearing a leather jacket and I thought: poser. *(Sean Hughes)*

They're going to put you away for so many years that, the next time you see Belfast, they'll be running day trips to the moon. *(Detective to the wrongfully accused Guildford Four victim, Gerry Conlon, in 1989)*

I don't get ulcers; I give them. *(Ed Koch)*

Marshall McLuhan hits a very large nail not quite on the head. *(Kenneth Boulding)*

Equality means you're just as good as the next man, but the next man is not half as good as you are. *(George Mikes)*

The typewriter, 1/2ike all mac&hines, has amind of it sown. *(A.P. Herbert)*

In 1913 science decided that there were such things as vitamins. Before then, people had just been eating food. *(Robert Benchley)*

Dancing with her was like moving a piano. *(Ring Lardner, on an aquaintence)*

My experience of gentlemen's agreements is that, when it comes to the pinch, there are rarely enough bloody gentlemen about. *(Joseph Chifley)*

Middle age is when your old classmates are so grey and wrinkled and bald that they don't recognise you. *(Bennett Cerf)*

I have never killed a man, but I have read many obituaries with a lot of pleasure. *(Clarence Darrow)*

One good thing about being a hippie: you'll never miss an important phone call because you're in the bathtub. *(Steve Davis)*

One psychiatrist I know uses shock treatment. He gives you the bill in advance. *(Harry Hershfield)*

My next door neighbour is a real grouch. If she were an island, she'd fight with the water. *(Bob Hope)*

I'll give you an idea how crime-ridden our neighbourhood is. The other day I saw half a cop. *(Milton Berle)*

Husbands are like fires. They go out when unattended. *(Zsa-Zsa Gabor)*

Who says we didn't have controversial subjects on TV back then? Remember 'Bonanza'? It was about three guys in high heels living together. *(Milton Berle)*

Men love war because it's the one thing that stops women laughing at them. *(John Fowles)*

The last day my mother-in-law called, the mice threw themselves on the traps. *(Les Dawson)*

Modern journalists always apologise to one in private for what they have written against one in public. *(Oscar Wilde)*

People need two kinds of acquaintances, one to complain to while they boast to the other. *(Logan Pearsall Smith)*

I'll give you ten grand NOT to get out of bed. *(Irish chat show host Pat Kenny to rotund comedienne Dawn French apropos a discussion of supermodels who commanded that fee to leave their boudoirs every day).*

How did Helen Keller's parents punish her when she misbehaved? By rearranging the furniture. *(Graffito)*

He's the sort of man who will sit on a fire and then complain that his bottom is burning. *(W.S. Gilbert)*

If I had a head like yours, I'd have it circumcised. *(Dave Allen, to a heckler once)*

What are you going to do for a face when King Kong wants his arse back? *(Billy Connolly, to a heckler once)*

If I'm going to shoot a man, I prefer to sneak up behind him rather than have him agonise-over watching me coming from the front. *(Sir Gordon White, former chairman of Hanson industries)*

No healthy male ever really thinks or talks of anything save himself. *(H.L. Mencken)*

There are three kinds of intelligence: the intelligence of man, the intelligence of the animal, and the intelligence of the military. In that order. *(Gottfried Reinhardt)*

If Quentin Crisp had never existed, it's unlikely that anyone would have the nerve to invent him. *(The Times)*

Cecil Beaton's baroque is worse than his bite. *(Hank Brennan)*

If you think squash is a competitive activity, try flower arrangement. *(Alan Bennet)*

Better murder an infant in its cradle than nurse an unacted desire. *(William Blake)*

Getting an award from TV is like getting kissed by someone with bad breath. *(Mason Williams)*

To appreciate newspapers you have to read between the lies. *(Goodman Ace)*

Never trust men with short legs. Their brains are too near their bottoms. *(Noel Coward)*

Television is now so hungry for material they're scraping the *top* of the barrel. *(Gore Vidal)*

He not only overflowed with learning, but stood in the slop. *(Sydney Smith, on an enemy)*

I have the typical Irish relationship with my folks. I love them, but I don't particularly like them. *(Sean Hughes)*

One should forgive one's enemies, but not before they're hanged.
(Heinrich Heine)

A yuppie wouldn't salute the flag unless he was sure it was 100% cotton. *(Mark Russell)*

He had a face like a plateful of mortal sins. *(Brendan Behan)*

A visitor from Mars could easily pick out the civilised nations. They have the best implements of war. *(Herbert Prochnow)*

My guess is that 80% of the human race goes through life without having a single original thought. *(H.L. Mencken)*

Man is born a liar. Otherwise he would not have invented the proverb, 'Tell the truth and shame the devil'. *(Liam O'Flaherty)*

Psychology is as unnecessary as directions for using poison. *(Karl Kraus)*

Queen Elizabeth is the head of a dysfunctional family. If she lived on a council estate in Sheffield, she'd probably be put in council care. *(Michael Parkinson)*

I loathe people who keep dogs. They're coward's who haven't got the guts to bite themselves. *(August Strindberg)*

Why were men invented? Because a dildo can't take a dog for a walk. *(Jim Davison)*

Doctors pour drugs of which they know little, to cure diseases of which they know less, into human beings of which they know nothing. *(Voltaire)*

I believe in white supremacy until the blacks are educated to a point of responsibility. *(John Wayne)*

Never speak ill of yourself: your friends will always say enough on that subject. *(Charles Talleyrand)*

The public is wonderfully tolerant. It forgives everything except genius. *(Oscar Wilde)*

Cough and the world coughs with you. Fart and you fart alone. *(Trevor Griffiths)*

Every dentist I have ever met has had thick wrists, black nazi hair on his arms and an ovaltine belly warming with the hymns of rats. *(Charles Bukowski)*

A prisoner of war is someone who tries to kill you, fails, and then asks you not to kill him. *(Winston Churchill)*

If it's abuse, one is always sure to hear of it from one damned good-natured friend or another. *(R.B. Sheridan)*

Rupert Murdoch's idea of a better world is a world that's better for Rupert. *(Ted Turner)*

It is better to give than to lend, and it costs about the same. *(Philip Gibbs)*

Heroin cheers me up for the brainlessness of people. *(Kurt Cobain)*

A foreign correspondent is someone who flies around from hotel to hotel and thinks that the most interesting thing about any story is the fact that he has arrived to cover it. *(Tom Stoppard)*

Terry has become a household word like sink tidy or waste disposal unit. He's nature's answer to insomnia. *(Alasdair Milne on Terry Wogan)*

There are worse things in life than death. Have you ever spent an evening with an insurance salesman? *(Woody Allen)*

My hometown is so dull the drugstore sells picture postcards of other towns. *(Milton Berle)*

The last time he was in hospital, he got Get Well cards from the nurses. *(Don Rickles)*

Most vegetarians I ever saw looked enough like their food to be classed as cannibals. *(Finley Peter Dunne)*

I was born by Caesarean section. That was the last time I had my mother's undivided attention. *(Richard Jeni)*

Richard Whiteley has brought bumbling incompetence and dreadful comic timing to a fine art. *(Terry Wogan on the 'Countdown' host)*

If you had a brain cell, it would die of loneliness. *(David Icke to Richard Littlejohn)*

My grandmother took a bath every year, whether she was dirty or not. *(Brendan Behan)*

A bulldog on valium. *(Brian Boyd on Jack Dee)*

All I can say about the drug culture is: plenty of drugs but not much culture. *(Brian Epstein)*

The writers and designers of *'Spitting Image'* should be unmercifully sued for making the royal family seem generally more intelligent and attractive than they actually are. *(Morrissey)*

Why is it that overweight people wear track suits? Do they feel this gives them the appearance of being fit and sporty? The gut may be huge, but the track suit somehow proves they're still in touch with their bodies, even if they haven't seen their genitalia for a month. *(Tony Hawks)*

My main education took place on the holidays from Eton. *(Osbert Sitwell)*

Peter Cook regretted nothing about his life. Except, perhaps, on one occasion in America when he saved David Frost from drowning. *(Alan Bennett)*

It's always better to leave people pissed off, they deserve it. Just be kind to the caterpillar and the moth and the gods will smile at you. *(Charles Bukowski)*

Queen Anne was meekly stupid when in good humour, and when in bad humour sulkily stupid. *(Thomas Babington Macaulay)*

Physically there is nothing to distinguish human society from the farmyard except that children are more troublesome and costly than chickens, and women are not so completely enslaved as farm stock. *(George Bernard Shaw)*

Once a newspaper touches a story, the facts are lost forever, even to the protagonists. *(Norman Mailer)*

She has only one fault: she is insufferable. *(Napoleon on Madame de Stael)*

Bernard Shaw went to church the other day and when they passed him the plate, moved aside murmuring 'press'. *(Oliver St. John Gogarty)*

History is a nightmare from which I am trying to awake. *(James Joyce)*

A virus is only doing its job. *(David Cronenberg)*

My wife is so fat that everytime she gets into a cab, the driver rushes her to the hospital. *(Dave Barry)*

Why do bald people insist on wearing ponytails? From the back it looks like a cat got stuck up the Christmas turkey. *(Jaspar Carrott)*

My dad was the town drunk. Usually that's not so bad...but New York city? *(Henny Youngman)*

I have never known an auctioneer to lie unless it was absolutely necessary. *(Josh Billings)*

An abstainer is the sort of man you wouldn't want to drink with even if you did. *(George Jean Nathan)*

He gave a moving speech. Long before he finished, his audience had moved out into the hall. *(Peter Shaw)*

The bubonic plagiarist. *(Jonathan Miller on David Frost)*

The unspeakable in pursuit of the uneatable. *(Oscar Wilde on fox-hunting)*

You look like an Easter Island statue with an arse full of razor blades. *(Paul Keating to Malcolm Fraser)*

Nothing is so silly as the expression of a man who's being complimented. *(Andre Gide)*

Many people have equated the intelligence of the dolphin with that of man. I'm afraid that, in the comparison, the dolphin comes of rather badly. *(Richard Harris)*

A single sentence will suffice for modern man: he fornicated and read the newspapers. *(Albert Camus)*

Advertisements contain the only truths to be relied on in a newspaper. *(Thomas Jefferson)*

I've never met anyone who supports royalty except some deaf and elderly pensioner in Hartlepool who has pictures of Prince Edward pinned on the toilet seat. *(Morrissey)*

Throughout the greater part of his life, George 111 was a kind of consecrated obstruction. *(Walter Bagehot)*

A hippie is someone who looks like Tarzan, walks like Jane, and smells like Cheetah. *(Ronald Reagan)*

If you pick up a starving dog and make him prosperous he will not bite you. That is the principal difference between a dog and a man. *(Mark Twain)*

The family is the last hiding place of the ultimate fool *(Charles Bukowski)*

A pig, an ass, a dunghill, the spawn of an adder, a basilisk, a lying buffoon, a mad fool with a frothy mouth, a lubberly ass. *(Martin Luther in subdued mood describing Henry Vlll)*

Life doesn't imitate art. It imitates bad television. *(Woody Allen)*

The trouble with Freud is that he never played the Glasgow Empire Saturday night. *(Les Dodd)*

You're so crooked, if you swallowed a nail you'd shit a corkscrew. *(Sir Gerald Templar to Lord Mountbatten)*

Nobody knows anything. *(William Goldman)*

I've just heard about his illness. Let's hope it's nothing trivial. *(Irvin Cobb)*

Somebody else's.
(Diogenes, after being asked what wine he liked best)

If some people got their rights they would complain of being deprived of their wrongs. *(Oliver Herford)*

I get my exercise acting as pallbearer to friends who exercise. *(Chancey Depew)*

Everybody winds up kissing the wrong person goodnight. *(Andy Warhol)*

Don't just stand there - undo something. *(Bob Hope to the stripper Gypsy Rose Lee)*

An editor admitted to me recently that a TV critic's function is merely to confirm the viewer in their prejudices. *(Terry Wogan)*

Men are generally assholes. *(Liam Neeson)*

I like to tease my plants: I water them with ice cubes. *(Steven Wright)*

The only real worry I have about going to prison is the thought of Lord Longford coming to visit me. *(Ex 'Private Eye' editor Richard Ingrams when such a prospect loomed during a court action against his publication).*

He was born silly and had a relapse. *(Arthur Baer)*

How much would you charge to haunt a house? *(Arthur Baer)*

Never offend people with style when you can offend them with substance. *(Sam Brown)*

Young gorillas are friendly - but they soon learn. *(Will Cuppy)*

Do you think it important to be nice to people on the way up in case you meet them again on the way down? Heaven help you. That is the sort of stupid, wimpy, namby-pamby attitude that will keep you sitting behind that cheap laminated teak desk of yours for the rest of what you laughingly call your career. *(Alexander Prosser)*

I love long walks, especially when they're taken by people who annoy me. *(Fred Allen)*

The man recovered of the bite. The dog it was that died. *(Oliver Goldsmith)*

He was a great patriot, a humanitarian, a loyal friend-provided of course, that he really is dead. *(Voltaire at an acquaintances graveside)*

And you lived to tell the tale? *(Prince Charles to a woman who said she had once met Princess Diana)*

What's on your mind, if you'll forgive the overstatement. *(Fred Allen)*

Things that are said to do one good generally taste of sawdust and burnt rubber. *(R.W.B. Howarth)*

No doubt Jack the Ripper excused himself on the grounds that it was human nature. *(A.A.Milne)*

Many of us believe in trying to make other people happy only if they can be happy in ways which we approve. *(Robert S. Lynd)*

A cocktail party is a gathering where sandwiches and friends are cut into little pieces. *(Milton Berle)*

I am unable to accept owing to a subsequent engagement. *(Oscar Wilde refusing an invitation to dine with an acquaintance he disliked)*

The man was so small, he was a waste of skin. *(Fred Allen)*

Never in the history of fashion has so little material been raised so high to reveal so much that needs to be covered so badly. *(Cecil Beaton on the mini-skirt)*

Gynaecologists, look up a friend today. *(Bruce Ridley)*

Moral indignation is jealousy with a halo. *(H.G. Wells)*

If the grass is greener in the other fellows yard let him worry about cutting it. *(Fred Allen)*

Very sorry can't come. Lie follows by post. *(Lord Charles Beresford refusing an invitation to dine with the Prince of Wales by telegram)*

Whenever I pick someone up hitch-hiking I always like to wait a few minutes before I say anything to them. Then I say, 'So how far did you think you were going? Put your seatbelt on - I wanna try something. I saw it in a cartoon but I'm pretty sure I can do it.' *(Steven Wright)*

When I say 'Everybody says so', I mean I say so. *(Ed Howe)*

A realist is a man who is about to do something he's ashamed of. *(Sydney Harris)*

A fine friend is one who stabs you in the front. *(Leonard Levinson)*

If we were to wake up some morning and find that everyone was the same race, the same creed and colour, we would find some other causes for prejudice by noon. *(George Aiken)*

Early to rise and early to bed, makes a man healthy, wealthy and dead. *(James Thurber)*

We forfeit three-quarters of ourselves in order to be like other people. *(Arthur Schopenhauer)*

She has that many double chins, she looks like she's staring out over the top of a sliced loaf. *(Roy Brown)*

If we all said to people's faces what we say behind one another's backs, society would be impossible. *(Honore de Balzac)*

I didn't spend 25 years getting to where I am so that you assholes could make a living off me. Why don't you all go fuck yourselves. *(Don Henley to a group of photographers who were annoying him)*

The Kray twins are legends in their own life sentences. *(Robert King)*

We're weathering a period of low mortality well, but it will tail off. People can't live forever. *(Funeral executive Eric Spencer)*

Could one enter a plea of justifiable homicide for decapitating oafs who come unbidden and sit beside one in pubs in the sacred hour between five and six pm? *(Hugh Leonard)*

You're looking nicer than usual, but then that's easy for you. *(Saki)*

You can catch more things in doctor's waiting rooms than you go in with. *(Mike Harding)*

I'd rather be an opportunist and float than go to the bottom with my principles round my neck. *(Stanley Baldwin)*

Man is the only animal of prey that is sociable. Every one of us preys upon his neighbour, and yet we herd together. *(John Gay)*

He's such an old bore, even the grave yawns for him. *(Herbert Beerbohm Tree on Israel Zangwill)*

The classic definition of chutzpah is the man who killed his parents and then threw himself at the mercy of the court on the grounds that he was an orphan. *(Leo Rosten)*

I left *The Sunday Press* to go into journalism. *(Kevin Marron)*

Her heart is in the right place. It's a pity the other fifteen stone isn't. *(Bob Monkhouse)*

We've had bad luck with our children, they've all grown up. *(Christopher Morley)*

Lager is a brown liquid for people who like to look as though they're drinking beer but don't like the taste. *(Kenneth Clarke)*

As soon as one is unhappy, one becomes moral. *(Marcel Proust)*

You can't think rationally on an empty stomach - and a whole lot of people can't do it on a full one either. *(Lord Reith)*

He had a chin on which large numbers of hairs weakly curled and clustered to cover its retreat. *(Max Beerbohm)*

Don't jump on a man unless he's down.
(Finley Peter Dunne)

Everything is funny as long as its happening to someone else. *(Will Rogers)*

Man is the only animal who causes pain to others with no other object than wanting to do so.
(Arthur Schopenhauer)

One should always play fairly when one has the winning cards. *(Oscar Wilde)*

The bloom of her ugliness is going off. *(Courtier of King George on Queen Charlotte Sophia's improvement with age)*

He is as good as his word - but his word is no good. *(Seamus McManus)*

The closest to perfection a man ever comes is when he fills out a job application form. *(Nicolas Chamfort)*

On my gravestone I'd like them to say, 'He didn't know what he was doing'. *(Terry Wogan)*

The main reason a chap becomes a bookmaker is because he's too scared to steal and too heavy to become a jockey. *(Gordon Richards)*

A Smith & Wesson beats four aces. *(Michael Enright)*

Express a mean opinion of yourself occasionally; it will show your friends that you know how to tell the truth. *(Ed Howe)*

Jimmy Hoffa's most valuable contribution to the American labour movement came at the moment he stopped breathing on July 3 1975. *(Dan Moldea)*

The only thing your friends will never forgive you for is your happiness. *(Albert Camus)*

This is the first age that has paid such attention to the future, which is rather ironic, since we may not have one. *(Arthur C. Clarke)*

One-fifth of the people are against everything all the time. *(Robert Kennedy)*

The Billy Carter of the British monarchy. *(Robert Lacey on Princess Margaret)*

Ten years ago the moon was an inspiration to poets and an opportunity for lovers. Ten years from now it will be just another airport. *(Emmanuel Mesthene)*

A healthy male adult bore consumes one and a half times his own weight in other people's patience. *(John Updike)*

Anyone informed that the universe is expanding and contracting in pulsations of eighty billion years has a right to ask, 'What's in it for me?' *(Peter de Vries)*

To err is human. To really foul things up requires a computer. *(Philip Howard)*

I used to take Dexamyl to give me enough confidence to start work. Now I take it to give me enough confidence not to. *(Kenneth Tynan)*

College is a place where we pass from adolescence to adultery. *(Ronald Berry)*

She uttered a sound rather like an elephant taking its foot out of a mud hole in a Burmese teak forest. *(P.G. Wodehouse)*

If it squirms it's biology. If it stinks it's chemistry. If it doesn't work it's physics - and if you can't understand it, it's mathematics. *(Magnus Pyke)*

You can't say civilisation don't advance, for in every war they kill you in a new way. *(Will Rogers)*

The truth which makes men free is for the most part the truth which men prefer not to hear. *(Herbert Agar)*

A great many people think they are thinking when they are merely re-arranging their prejudices. *(William James)*

It's difficult to say anything nice about broccoli except that it has no bones. *(Johnny Martin)*

The only thing that saves us from bureaucracy is its inefficiency. *(Eugene McCarthy)*

Cultivate what the public does not like about you. That is who you are. *(Jean Cocteau)*

Awards are like haemorrhoids. In the end, every asshole gets one. *(Frederic Raphael)*

I hope this won't spoil y'all's trading day. *(Deranged killer Mark Barton in an Atlanta financial centre in July 1999 before blowing away nine people)*

The only thing you can believe in a newspaper is the date. *(J.B.S. Haldane)*

If you want to get rid of somebody, just tell them something for their own good. *(Kin Hubbard)*

To his dog. every man is Napoleon. Hence the constant popularity of dogs. *(Aldous Huxley)*

A doorman is a genius who opens your taxi door with one hand, helps you in with the other, and still has a hand left waiting for the tip. *(Earl Wilson)*

It's going to be fun to see how long the meek can hold on to the earth after they inherit it. *(Dan Quinn)*

Asthma is a disease that has practically the same symptoms as passion, except for the fact that it lasts longer. *(Rodney Dangerfield)*

Since he started to wear a pacemaker, every time he makes love his garage door opens. *(Stuart Turner)*

I don't like people who can't sit still for half an hour without a drink in their hands, but I would still prefer an amiable drunk to Henry Ford. *(Raymond Chandler)*

We have three kinds of friends: those who love us, those who are indifferent to us, and those who hate us.
(Nicolas de Chamfort)

When you were young the Dead Sea was only sick. *(George Burns to Bob Hope)*

The next time anyone asks you, 'What is Bertrand Russell's philosophy?' The correct answer is, 'What year. please?' *(Sydney Hook)*

For seventeen years he did nothing but kill animals and stick in stamps. *(Harold Nicolson on King George V)*

There's nothing sooner dries than a woman's tears. *(John Webster)*

Journalists are people who take in another's washing and then sell it. *(Barnard Eldershaw)*

He had a pair of buck teeth that made him look like the first cousin of a walrus. *(Richard Brautigan)*

Posterity will ne'er survey
A nobler grave than this;
Here lies the bones Castlereagh:
Stop, traveller, and piss.
(Lord Byron's affectionate epitaph to Viscount Castlereagh)

My wife wanted a foreign convertible for her birthday. I got her a rickshaw. *(Henny Youngman)*

She wears her clothes as if they were thrown over her with a pitchfork. *(Jonathan Swift)*

The Queen is a piece of cardboard they drag round on a trolley. *(Johnny Rotten)*

The great BBC maxim is, 'If it ain't broke - break it. *(Terry Wogan)*

Your solemn mug is so like an old peasant woman's arse; all it asks for is to be kicked. *(Alexander Pushkin to Ivan Lanov)*

Trust him as much as you would a rattlesnake with a silencer on its rattle. *(Dean Acheson on J. Edgar Hoover)*

I now know why Prince Charles spent so much of his time talking to vegetables: he knew he would get more sense out of them than the fruit he married. *(Andrew Morton on Lady Di in 1997. He revised this view somewhat after she died).*

He must have been an incredibly good shot. *(Noel Coward upon hearing an intellectually-challenged actor had put a bullet through his brain)*

You can get more with a kind word and a gun than you can with a kind word. *(Johnny Carson)*

The theories of Einstein are merely the ravings of a mind polluted with liberal and democratic nonsense. *(Walter Gross in 1936)*

Universities are like old people's homes - except that more people actually die in universities. *(Bob Dylan)*

You're such a pain in the arse you make piles seem like a gift from fucking heaven. *(Lee Dunne)*

The only time I ever heard the Fishers say anything kind about my mother was in the limousine on the way to her funeral. *(Eddie Fisher)*

An enormous two or three mile ditch, running liquid mud. *(Charles Dickens on the Mississippi river)*

If sunbeams were weapons of war, we would have had solar energy long ago. *(George Porter)*

Stephen Fry has all the wit of an unflushed toilet. *(Bernard Manning)*

I was brought up to respect my elders, but now I don't have to respect anybody. *(George Burns at 87)*

In a rage, Alexander Woolcott has all the tenderness and restraint of a newly caged cobra. *(Noel Coward)*

He's completely unspoiled by failure. *(Noel Coward on a colleague)*

The people who live in a Golden Age usually go around complaining how yellow everything looks. *(Randall Jarrell)*

It is better to waste one's youth than do nothing with it at all. *(Georges Courteline)*

Parents are sometimes a bit of a disappointment to their children. They don't fulfill the promise of their early years. *(Anthony Powell)*

When you've seen a nude infant doing a backward somersault you know why clothing exists. *(Stephen Fry)*

All the individuals within the Royal Family, they're so magnificently, unaccountably and unpardonably boring. *(Morrissey)*

The men who really believe in themselves are all in lunatic asylums. *(G.K. Chesterton)*

Princess Diana never uttered one statement that has been of any use to any member of the human race. *(Morrissey)*

The Concorde is so fast it gives you an extra few hours to lose your luggage. *(Bob Hope)*

Lester Piggott has a face like a well-kept grave. *(Jack Leach)*

It takes two to make a murder. There are people born to have their throats cut. *(Aldous Huxley)*

Be nice to people on the way up because you'll meet'em on the way down as well. *(Wilson Mizner)*

The stores are full of fantastic junk and everything you want is out of stock. People with strained, agonised expressions are poring over pieces of distorted glass and pottery and being waited on by specially recruited morons on temporary parole from mental institutions, some of whom by determined effort can tell a teapot from a pickaxe. *(Raymond Chandler on Christmas)*

What we need is hatred. From it are our ideas born. *(Jean Genet)*

He was dressed in a barrage balloon, cleverly painted to look like a dinner jacket. *(Clive James)*

Manners are especially the need of the plain. The pretty can get away with anything. *(H.G. Wells)*

Laughter would be bereaved if snobbery died. *(Peter Ustinov)*

Pubs make you as drunk as they can as soon as they can, and turn nasty when they succeed *(Colin MacInnes)*

Bores can be divided into two classes: those who have their own particular subject, and those who do not need a subject. *(A.A. Milne)*

The smartest thing I ever heard Chris Evans say was 'Good morning'. *(Spike Milligan)*

Time is a great teacher, but unfortunately it kills all its pupils. *(Hector Berlioz)*

I'm not saying he was lazy, but he used to ride his bike over cobblestones to knock the ash off his ciggie.
(Les Dawson)

In America, while there's someone on every street corner trying to convince you to eat yourself into oblivion, there is also another kindly soul ready to sell you the most effective diet in the history of the world. *(Mark Little)*

We can't stand around here doing nothing, you know. People will think we're workmen. *(Spike Milligan)*

He was a self-made man who owed his lack of success to nobody. *(Joe Heller)*

If you want to keep something concealed from your enemy, do not disclose it to your friend. *(Solomon Gabirol)*

One of the most pleasing sounds of springtime is the contented cooing of osteopaths as Man picks up his garden spade. *(Oliver Pritchett)*

If one hides one's talents under a bushel, one must be careful to point out to everyone the exact bushel under which it is hidden. *(Saki)*

I always pass on good advice. It is the only thing to do with it. It is never any use to oneself. *(Oscar Wilde)*

The disease of niceness cripples more lives than alcoholism. *(Robin Chandler)*

Mistrust first impulses: they are always good. *(Charles de Talleyrand)*

Of course I have standards. They may be low, but I have them. *(Yogi Berra)*

We should be thankful to lynch mobs. I've got a brother who can run a half-mile faster than any white boy in the world. *(Dick Gregory)*

Vegetarians have weak, shifty eyes and laugh in a cold, calculating manner. They drink water, steal stamps and pinch little children. *(J.B. Morton)*

Princess Diana looked like an incredible cocker spaniel. *(Robin Williams)*

His smile looks like a crowded graveyard with the gate left open. *(Red Skelton on David Letterman)*

Television is a medium that has raised writing to a new low. *(Samuel Goldwyn)*

There are two things for which animals are to be envied: they know nothing of future evils, or of what people say about them. *(Voltaire)*

Jonathan Ross is the sinking man's David Letterman. *(Garry Bushell)*

When you get your hospital bill you understand why surgeons wear masks in the operating room. *(Sam Levenson)*

It was like having a glass of wine. *(Mafia contract killer Ray Ferrito explaining how he felt after killing a rival hood).*

Would you ever buy a used car from me? *(John de Lorean)*

When I hear anyone talk of culture I reach for my revolver. *(Hans Johst)*

I love you so much I named my first ulcer after you. *(Les Dawson)*

Charity begins at home - and usually stays there. *(Elbert Hubbard)*

Like a Goth swaggering round Rome wearing an onyx toilet seat for a collar, he exudes self-confidence. *(Clive James on Rupert Murdoch)*

Manners are the lowest common denominator of ethical experience. *(Victor Navasky)*

If a man's character is to be abused, there's nobody like a relation to do the business. *(William Makepeace Thackeray)*

Oh, the self-importance of fading stars. Never mind, they will be black holes one day. *(Jeffrey Barnard)*

When I die. I want to decompose in a barrel of porter and have it served in all the pubs in Dublin. *(J.P. Donleavy)*

Shame is the feeling you have when you agree with the woman who loves you that you are the man she thinks you are. *(Carl Sandburg)*

If at first you don't succeed, pry, pry again. *(Philip MacDonald)*

Perfection is such a nuisance that I often regret having cured myself of using tobacco. *(Emile Zola)*

No one gossips about other people's secret virtues. *(Bertrand Russell)*

Let's banish bridge and find a more pleasant way of being miserable together. *(Don Herold)*

A computer once beat me at chess, but it was no match for me at kick-boxing. *(Emo Philips)*

Keeping up with the Joneses was a full-time job with my mother and father. It was not until many years later when I lived alone that I realised how much cheaper it was to drag the Joneses down to my level. *(Quentin Crisp)*

Everybody hates me because I'm so universally liked. *(Peter de Vries)*

Investigative journalism consists of putting a well-known figure on a spit and getting the public to turn him. *(George Bernard Shaw)*

A dreamer is someone who notices that a rose smells better than a cabbage, and thereby concludes that it will also make better soup. *(H.L. Mencken)*

A stupid man doing something he would otherwise be ashamed of always calls it his duty. *(George Bernard Shaw)*

Egotism is the anaesthetic that dulls the pain of stupidity. *(Frank Leahy)*

Oratory is the art of making deep noises from the chest sound like important messages from the brain. *(H.I. Philips)*

Television: a medium which allows millions of people to listen to the same joke at the same time and still be lonely. *(T.S. Eliot)*

Technology is what happens when impossibility yields to necessity. *(Adlai Stevenson)*

Editors are people who separate the wheat from the chaff - and then print the chaff. *(Elbert Hubbard)*

I am more and more convinced that Scrooge was one of the most sensible men that I have ever read about. *(Michael Green)*

Suicide is belated acquiescence in the opinions of one's wife's relatives. *(H.L. Mencken)*

Conscience is the inner voice that warns us someone may be looking. *(H.L,. Mencken)*

Never strike anyone so old, small or weak that verbal abuse would have sufficed. *(P.J. O'Rourke)*

He has left his body to science, and science is contesting the will. *(David Frost)*

Men are the only animals that devote themselves assiduously to making one another unhappy. *(H.L. Mencken)*

Trust everybody, but cut the cards. *(Peter Finley Dunne)*

What is your host's purpose in having a party? Surely not for you to enjoy yourself. If that were their sole purpose, they'd simply have sent champagne and women over to your place by taxi. *(P.J. O'Rourke)*

My only criticism of Lord Longford is that he has a tendency to forgive people for things they didn't do to him. *(Brian Masters)*

I didn't know he'd been knighted. I knew he'd been doctored. *(Thomas Beecham on Malcolm Sargent)*

American football makes rugby look like a Tupperware Party. *(Sue Lawley)*

The dullard's envy of brilliant men is always assuaged by the suspicion that they will come to a bad end. *(Sir Max Beerbohm)*

Any fool can tell the truth, but it requires a man of some sense to know how to lie well. *(Samuel Butler)*

I would never work in television. I don't want my audience going for a piss or making tea while I'm hard at work. *(Dirk Bogarde)*

If you're not cynical, you're stupid. *(Paul Zimmerman)*

Queen Victoria was an amiable field-mouse. *(James Pope-Hennessy)*

To have a grievance is to have a purpose in life. *(Eric Hoffer)*

You will always stay young if you live honestly, eat slowly, sleep sufficiently, work industriously, worship faithfully - and lie about your age. *(Bob Hope)*

Prince Charles is the only member of the Royal Family who ever left Cinderella for the Ugly Duckling. *(Des Hanafin)*

I bomb, therefore I am.
(Philip Slater)

I hate to advocate drugs, alcohol violence or insanity to anyone, but they've always worked for me. *(Hunter S. Thompson)*

Forgive your enemies, but never forget their names. *(John F. Kennedy)*

You should always persuade decision-makers that the decision you want is their idea. *(Michael Shea, former press secretary to the Queen)*

When you have done a fault, be always pert and insolent and behave as if you yourself were the injured party. *(Jonathan Swift)*

I have invented rubber food for old-people with time to kill. *(Pat McCormick)*

At one time an organisation called Alcoholics Unanimous was established in Dublin but its membership fell away and it wasn't worth while to prop them up against the bar counter again. *(Tony Butler)*

Milton Berle is the thief of bad gags. *(Walter Winchell)*

Shut up that goddam crying. I won't have brave men here who have been shot seeing a yellow bastard crying. You're going back to the frontlines and you may get shot and killed, but you're going to fight. If you don't I'll stand you up against a wall and have a firing squad kill you on purpose. I ought to do it myself, you goddam whimpering coward. *(George Patton to a shell-shocked soldier in hospital during World War Two.)*

There's nobody as daft as an educated man once you get him off the subject he was educated in. *(Owen Kelly)*

To some extent I'm sad I didn't have a university education. However, I have come across so many people with degrees who are as thick as planks I have largely lost that resentment. *(Gay Byrne)*

I think it would be a good idea. *(Gandhi's reply when asked what he thought of western civilisation)*

If some great catastrophe is not announced every morning in the newspapers, we feel a certain void. *(Paul Valery)*

To the puritan, all things are impure. *(D.H. Lawrence)*

Middle age is when you've met so many people that every new person you meet reminds you of someone else, and usually is. *(Ogden Nash)*

Animals have three advantages over men: they have no theologians to instruct them, their funerals cost them nothing, and no one starts lawsuits over their wills. *(Voltaire)*

Puritans hate bear-baiting not because it gives pain to the bear but because it gives pleasure to the spectators. *(Thomas Macaulay)*

What you don't know would make a great book. *(Sydney Smith)*

My doctor is wonderful. Once when I couldn't afford an operation, he touched up the X-rays. *(Joey Bishop)*

The gods have bestowed on Max Beerbohm the gift of perpetual old age. *(Oscar Wilde)*

Laugh and the world laughs with you; snore and you snore alone. *(Anthony Burgess)*

An ambassador is an honest man sent abroad to lie for his country. *(Henry Wooton)*

You don't have to think too hard when you talk to a teacher. *(J.D. Salinger)*

The two main people you lie to in your life are your girlfriend and the police. *(Jack Nicholson)*

To feel themselves in the presence of greatness, many men find it necessary only to be alone. *(Tom Masson)*

Santa Claus is the only guy who knows how to solve the world's problems and yet doesn't want to be president. *(Herbert Prochnow)*

Never complain. Never explain. Get even. *(Robert Kennedy)*

How fond men are of justice when it comes to judging the crimes of former generations. *(Armand Salacrou)*

Give me a home where the buffaloes roam and I'll show you a housefull of dirt. *(Marty Allen)*

Talking to journalists is like screwing in public. *(Sean Connery)*

Progress is really just the exchange of one nuisance for another. *(Havelock Ellis)*

Muesli is like designer vomit. *(Jasper Carrott)*

May the Lamb of God stick his hind leg out through the golden canopy of heaven and kick the bollox off ye. *(Stephen Behan, the father of Brendan, to a man who spilled a pint of beer over him one time).*

On hearing of the death of anyone I've known well, I've usually experienced a slight thrill of pleasure. *(Quentin Crisp)*

Paul Johnson looks like an explosion in a pubic hair factory. *(Jonathan Miller)*

Television isn't interested in ideas. It employs people who cannot think. TV people keep saying 'Where are the pictures?' If Jesus Christ came back to this planet and agreed to do an interview on 'Everyman', they'd say, 'He's an outstanding talking head, but where are the pictures?' *(John Cleese)*

I wish you were a statue and I was a pigeon. *(Don Rickles)*

Hate makes the world go round. *(Morrissey)*

No self-respecting fish would be wrapped in a Murdoch newspaper *(Mike Royko)*

Only his varicose veins save him from being completely colourless. *(Hal Roach)*

There's no other living creature that's as wicked as man. Animals never do the detestable, horrible things that human beings do. Can you imagine animals creating concentration camps and torturing people to death? Can you imagine animals with a capital punishment law running through the gorilla family? *(Truman Capote)*

He was so ugly when he was born that the doctor slapped his mother. *(Henny Youngman)*

The Queen Mother's greatest achievement in 101 years was not choking on a fishbone. *(Ian O'Doherty after that lady died in 2002).*

There is no spectacle more agreeable than to observe an old friend fall from a rooftop. *(Confucius)*

I'm pleading with my wife to have birthdays again. I don't want to grow old alone. *(Rodney Dangerfield)*

Mickey Rooney has to live to be 100 so he can pay the alimony he owes all those ex-wives. He's not ALLOWED to die. *(George Burns)*

On my 70th birthday I hung a black wreath on my door. *(Bette Davis)*

Yes, I'd consider going out with women my age - if there WERE any. *(George Burns at 92)*

I've been around so long I knew Doris Day before she was a virgin. *(Groucho Marx)*

Advanced old age is when you sit in a rocking chair and can't get it going. *(Eliakim Katz)*

Old age is the happiest time in a man's life. The trouble is, there's so little of it. *(W.S. Gilbert)*

I have no views. When one is retired it is sensible to refrain from having views. *(Joseph Alsop)*

For a while you're venerable; then you're, just old. *(Lance Alworth)*

The trouble is, you're not allowed to grow old in the world anymore. *(Tony Hancock)*

You can calculate Zsa Zsa Gabor's age by the rings on her fingers. *(Bob Hope)*

Anita Ekberg is the thinking man's dunce cap. Two of them. *(Ethel Merman)*

Growing old is like being increasingly penalised for a crime you haven't committed. *(Anthony Powell)*

I recently turned 60. Practically a third of my life is over. *(Woody Allen)*

When a man of 60 runs off with a young woman I wish him luck. After all, he's going to need it. *(Deborah Kerr)*

Getting on in years means suffering the morning after when you haven't even had the night before. *(Henny Youngman)*

He was either a man of about 150 who was rather young for his years or a man of about 110 who had been aged by trouble. *(P.G Wodehouse)*

If you can eat a boiled egg at 90 in England they think you deserve the Nobel Prize. *(Alan Bennett)*

If I'd known I was going to live this long I'd have taken better care of myself. *(Adolph Zukor)*

I've got to the age where I need my false teeth and my hearing aid before I can ask where I've left my glasses. *(Stuart Turner)*

He's so old that when he orders a 3-minute egg, they ask for the money upfront. *(Milton Berle)*

The only thing that bothers me about growing older is that when I see a pretty girl now it arouses my memory instead of my hopes. *(Milton Berle)*

There are so many ways of dying. It's astonishing that any of us choose old age. *(Beryl Bainbridge)*

I'm at the age where my back goes out more than I do. *(Phyllis Diller)*

I'm now at the age where I've got to prove that I'm just as good as I never was. *(Rex Harrison)*

People ought to retire at 40 when they feel over-used and go back to work at 65 when they feel useless. *(Carol Anne O'Marie)*

Madonna and Sean Penn were the beauty and the beast. But which was which? *(Joan Rivers)*

When Whoopi Goldberg wears a dress it's like drag. *(Mildred Natwick)*

She probably thinks Sinai is the plural of sinus. *(Joan Rivers on Bo Derek)*

Take away Julia Robert's wild mane of hair and all those teeth and elastic lips and what have you got? A pony! *(Joyce Haber)*

She looks like she combs her hair with an egg-beater. *(Louella Parsons on Joan Collins)*

'Hollywood is a place where the only thing an actor saves for a rainy day is someone else's umbrella'.*(Lynn Bari)*

'Hollywood believes it's better to have loved and divorced than never to have had any publicity at all'.*(Ava Gardner)*

'If someone were to come from another planet and see the world through movies, they'd think it was populated by white men in their thirties who shot a lot'.*(Bonnie Bedelia)*

'To have a vagina and a point of view in this town is a lethal combination'.
(Sharon Stone)

Hollywood is a place that attracts people with huge holes in their souls'.*(Julia Phillips)*

'Sex is God's biggest joke on human beings. *(Bette Davis)*

Men like to see women as objects: that image of totally contrived sexuality — bleached hair, pushed-up tits and make-up an inch thick—still works. *(Theresa Russell)*

He was a rather refined young man, who preferred sex dreams to visiting brothels, because he met a much nicer type of girl that way. *(Vivian Mercer)*

The trouble about most lovers is that they have a habit of turning into husbands. *(Diana Dors)*

There are a lot of more interesting things in life than sex. Gardening, for instance. *(Jean Alexander)*

Henry Kissinger's idea of sex was to slow down to 30 miles per hour when he dropped you off at the door. *(Barbara Howard)*

I don't spend too much time in Hollywood. I'm afraid I might wind up as one of Hugh Hefner's bunnies. *(Liv Ullmann)*

There are lots of chicks who get laid by the director who still don't get the part. *(Claudia Linnear)*

Sex is like washing your face. You do it because you have to. *(Sophia Loren)*

David used sex the way a cat sprays, to mark his territory. *(Angela Bowie)*

I read the book of Job last night. I don't think God comes well out of it. *(Virginia Woolf)*

Coitus is punishment. Marriage is legalised rape. Sex is power, nothing else. Romance is rape embellished with meaningful looks. *(Andrea Dworkin)*

Rod Stewart is so mean it hurts him to go to the toilet. *(Britt Ekland)*

Mick Jagger never knew how to shake that boney little ass of his until he watched me strut on stage. *(Tina Turner)*

It takes a great deal to produce ennui in an Englishman, and if you do, he only takes it as convincing proof that you are well-bred. *(Margaret Halsey)*

David wanted the basic, good old-fashioned English rock star marriage in which hubby lances his way boldly and beautifully around the globe, free as an eagle while wifey stays happily home on the nice suburban Home Counties estate, studying macrobiotics and macrame and raising babies in post-Woodstock Victorian virtue.. *(Angle Bowie)*

The majority of Irish men are bastards - and the majority of them are useless in bed. *(Mary Coughlan)*

'I'd never make another film rather than work with Otto Preminger. I don't think he could direct his little nephew to the bathroom'. *(Dyan Cannon)*

One writer I know has the unnerving habit of taking two extra copies of all his love letters - one for himself and the other for the British. Museum'.*(Jilly Cooper)*

To survive in Hollywood you need the ambition of a Latin-American revolutionary, the ego of a grand opera tenor...and the physical stamina of a cow pony. *(Billie Burke)*

When it's.3 o'clock in New York, it's still 1938 in London. *(Bette Midler)*

My main memory of 'Ryan's Daughter' is of sitting on a hilltop in a caravan at six in the morning in the pissing rain wondering what the hell I was doing there. *(Sarah Miles)*

A woman asking for equality in the church is equivalent to a black person demanding equality in the Ku Klux Klan. *(Mary Daly)*

Liz Taylor likes food so much she takes mayonnaise on her aspirins. *(Joan Rivers)*

My children never forgave me. Oedipus killed his father and married his mother, but I sold their Nintendo. *(Sue Arnold)*

You can say what you like about Genghis Khan but when he was around, old ladies could walk the streets of Mongolia at night *(Jo Brand)*

Adultery is the national sport of Cuba. *(Germaine Greer)*

If she stood beside a radiator she'd melt. *(Joan Rivers on Pamela Anderson)*

Ken is so tired his sperm are on crutches. *(Emma Thompson on her then husband Kenneth Branagh)*

My husband said he needed more space, so I locked him outside. *(Roseanne)*

It's a new low for actresses when we have to wonder what's between her ears instead of between her legs. *(Katharine Hepburn on Sharon Stone)*

Any woman who thinks marriage is a 50/50 proposition either doesn't understand men or percentages. *(Florynce Kennedy)*

To tell the honest truth, he's a lousy lay *(Carole Lombard on Clark Gable)*

Men hate to lose. I once beat my husband at tennis I asked him, 'Are we going to have sex again?' He said 'Yes, but not with each other.' *(Rita Rudner)*

I need a man in my house. To hook up the VCR and then leave. *(Joy Behar)*

In Hollywood a marriage is successful if it outlasts milk. *(Rita Rudner)*

Three wise men? You must be joking. *(Rita Rudner)*

Most earthquakes are caused by sudden movements of Roseanne Barr, *(Joan Rivers)*

I do a lot of reading on serial killers, mostly 'How To' Books. *(Roseanne Barr)*

A fag with pussy. *(Ava Gardner on Mia Farrow)*

When you start having lunch with your boyfriend and actually eating it, the relationship is already over. *(Erica Jong)*

Culturally and creatively, Jennifer Lopez is about as interesting as overheated meringue. *(Barbara Ellen)*

Men are brave enough to go to war, but not to get a bikini wax. *(Rita Rudner)*

Men don't get cellulite, which confirms my belief that God is, after all, male. *(Rita Rudner)*

Sex is for men, and marriage - like lifeboats - for women and children. *(Carrie fisher)*

'If a man does something silly, people say, 'Isn't he silly?' If a woman does something silly, people say, 'Aren't women silly?'. *(Doris Day)*

It wasn't a woman who betrayed Jesus with a kiss. *(Catherine Carswell)*

Woman have a lot of faults, but men only two: everything they say and everything they do. *(Leonora Strumpfenburg)*

More and more it appears that, biologically, men are destined for short brutal lives - and women for long, miserable ones *(Estelle Ramey)*

Their brains. *Dolores O' Riordan after being asked what was man's most useless invention)*

The male function is to produce sperm. we now have sperm banks. *(Valerie Solanas)*

The most fun part of being a feminist is scaring the shit out of men who are scumbags. *(Julie Birchill)*

'Princess Di wears more clothes in one day than Gandhi wore in his entire life.'*(Joan Rivers)*

'Modern drugs are wonderful. They enable a wife with pneumonia to nurse her husband through 'flu'. *(Jilly Cooper)*

'Let's face it: there are no plain women on television.' *(Anna Ford)*

'Children should be seen and not smelt.' *(Joyce Jillson)*

'After the rich, the most obnoxious people in the world are those that serve the rich'. *(Edna O'Brien)*

'Marion Davies has two expressions - joy and indigestion.' *(Dorothy Parker)*

'Millions long for eternity who wouldn't know what to do with themselves on a rainy Sunday afternoon.' *(Susan Ertz)*

'From the day she weighs 140 pounds, the chief excitement in a woman's life consists in spotting women who are fatter than she is.' *(Helen Rowland)*

'Girls wear less on the street today than their grandmothers did in bed'. *(Barbara Cartland)*

'The ultimate indignity is to be given a bedpan by a stranger who calls you by your first name.' *(Maggie Kuhn)*

I require only, 3 things in a man - that tie be handsome, ruthless.. .and stupid. *(Dorothy Parker)*

The more I think of men, the less I think of them. *(Anon)*

The first time Adam had a chance, he laid the blame on a woman. *(Nancy Astor)*

You see an awful lot of smart guys with dumb women, but you hardly ever a smart woman with a dumb guy. *(Erica Jong)*

People call me a feminist whenever I express sentiments that differentiate me from a doormat. *(Rebecca West)*

When you see what some girls marry, you realise how much they must hate to work for a living. *(Helen Rowland)*

Women Have a Lot of faults, but men have only two: everything they say and everything they do.
(Leonora Strumpfenburg)

Marriage is lonelier than solitude. *(Beverley Sills)*

The more I see of men, the more I admire dogs. *(Brigitte Bardot)*

Bing Crosby had the sticking-out ears of a pixie and the aloof demeanour of a camel. *(Ingrid Bergman)*

Yes I have acted with Clint Eastwood. Or rather I have acted opposite, Clint Eastwood. *(Geraldine Page)*

Gilbert Roland was a wonderful husband in one room of the house. *(Constance Bennett)*

Frederic March was able to do a very emotional scene with tears in his eyes and pinch my fanny at the same time. *(Shelley Winters)*

If my husband ever met a woman who looked like the ones in his paintings, he would fall over in a dead faint. *(Picasso's wife)*

Don't worry about Alan; he'll always land on somebody's feet. *(Dorothy Parker of her husband)*

He speaks to me as if I were a public meeting. *(Queen Victoria on Gladstone)*

George C. Scott: fine actor, big drinker, wife-beater. What else do you want to know? *(Colleen Dewhurst)*

Bobby Fischer is a chess phenomenon, it is true. But he's also a social illiterate, a political simpleton, a cultural ignoramus, and an emotional baby. *(Mary Kenny)*

Physical Love, forbidden as it was 20 or 30 years ago, has now become boringly obligatory. *(Francoise Sagan)*

By the time you say you're his/Shivering and sighing/And he vows his passion is/Infinite, undying - Lady make a note of this/One of you is lying. *(Dorothy Parker)*

If you never want to see a man again, say 'I love you. I want to marry you. I want to have children.' They leave skid marks. *(Rita Rudner)*

That youthful sparkle in his eyes is caused by his contact lenses which he keeps highly polished. *(Sheilah Graham on Ronald Reagan)*

'I do a lot of thinking about how I am going to merchandise my kids. Frankly, in clear conscience, I don't see how I can let them go into marriage without slapping a sticker on their foreheads that reads: This Person May Be Injurious to your Mental Health.' *(Erma Bormbeck)*

Nothing happened in our marriage. I nicknamed the water bed Lake Placid. *(Phyllis Diller)*

other POWERFRESH titles

POWERFRESH TONI GOFFE TITLES

1902929411	FINISHED AT 50	2.99 ☐
1902929403	FARTING	2.99 ☐
190292942X	LIFE AFTER BABY	2.99 ☐

POWERFRESH MAD SERIES

1874125783	MAD TO BE FATHER	2.99 ☐
1874125694	MAD TO BE A MOTHER	2.99 ☐
1874125686	MAD ON FOOTBALL	2.99 ☐
187412552X	MAD TO GET MARRIED	2.99 ☐
1874125546	MAD TO HAVE A BABY	2.99 ☐
1874125619	MAD TO HAVE A PONY	2.99 ☐
1874125627	MAD TO HAVE A CAT	2.99 ☐
1874125643	MAD TO BE 40 HIM	2.99 ☐
1874125651	MAD TO BE 40 HER	2.99 ☐
187412566X	MAD TO BE 50 HIM	2.99 ☐

POWERFRESH FUNNYSIDE SERIES

1874125260	FUNNY SIDE OF 30	2.99 ☐
1874125104	FUNNY SIDE OF 40 HIM	2.99 ☐
1874125112	FUNNY SIDE OF 40 HER	2.99 ☐
190292911X	FUNNY SIDE OF 50 HIM	2.99 ☐
1874125139	FUNNY SIDE OF 50 HER	2.99 ☐
1874125252	FUNNY SIDE OF 60	2.99 ☐
1874125279	FUNNY SIDE OF SEX	2.99 ☐

POWERFRESH OTHER A5

1874125171	"CRINKLED "N" WRINKLED"	2.99 ☐
1874125376	A MOTHER NO FUN	2.99 ☐
1874125449	WE'RE GETTING MARRIED	2.99 ☐
1874125481	CAT CRAZY	2.99 ☐
190292908X	EVERYTHING MEN KNOW ABOUT SEX	2.99 ☐
1902929071	EVERYTHING MEN KNOW ABOUT WMN	2.99 ☐
1902929004	KISSING COURSE	2.99 ☐
1874125996	CONGRATULATIONS YOU'VE PASSED	2.99 ☐
1902929276	TOILET VISITORS BOOK	2.99 ☐
1902929160	BIG FAT SLEEPY CAT	2.99 ☐

POWERFRESH SILVEY JEX TITLES

1902929055	FART ATTACK	2.99 ☐
1874125961	LOVE & PASSION 4 THE ELDERLY	2.99 ☐
187412597X	A BABY BOOK	2.99 ☐
1874125996	SHEEP 'N' NASTY	2.99 ☐
1874125988	SPORT FOR THE ELDERLY	2.99 ☐
1902929144	FUN & FROLICS FOR THE ELDERLY	2.99 ☐

POWERFRESH HUMOUR

1874125945	GUIDE TO SEX & SEDUCTION	3.99 ☐
1874125848	DICK'S NAUGHTY BOOK	3.99 ☐
190292925X	MODERN BABES LB OF SPELLS	4.99 ☐
1902929268	A MUMS LB OF SPELLS	4.99 ☐

POWERFRESH LITTLE SQUARE TITLES

1902929330	LS DIRTY JOKES	2.50 ☐
1902929314	LS DRINKING JOKES	2.50 ☐
1902929322	LS GOLF JOKES	2.50 ☐
190292939X	LS IRISH JOKES	2.50 ☐
1902929292	LS TURNING 18	2.50 ☐
1902929977	LS TURNING 21	2.50 ☐
1902929969	LS THE BIG 30	2.50 ☐
1902929241	LS THE BIG 40	2.50 ☐
1902929233	LS THE BIG 50	2.50 ☐
1902929284	LS BIG 60	2.50 ☐
1902929225	LS SINGLE V MARRIED WOMEN	2.50 ☐
1902929217	LS YES BUT...!	2.50 ☐
1902929306	LS WHISKY	2.50 ☐
1902929500	LS HOW TO PULL BY MAGIC	2.50 ☐

POWERFRESH STATIONARY TITLES

1902929381	WEDDING GUEST BOOK	9.99 ☐
1902929349	WEEKLY PLANNER CATS	6.99 ☐
1902929357	WEEKLY PLANNER DOGS	6.99 ☐
1902929365	WEEKLY PLANNER COTTAGES	6.99 ☐
1902929373	WEEKLY PLANNER OFFICE	6.99 ☐
1902929519	HUMDINGER TELEPHONE BOOK	4.99 ☐
1902929527	HUMDINGER ADDRESS BOOK	4.99 ☐
1902929535	HUMDINGER NOTEBOOK	2.99 ☐

Name

Address

P&P £1.00 Per Parcel

Please send cheques payable to Powerfresh LTD
To Powerfresh LTD 21 Rothersthorpe Crescent
Northampton NN4 8JD